# Cooking wi Celiac

## Hassle Free Celiac Recipes for Newly Diagnosed Celiac Patients

# Table of Contents

*Introduction* ........................................................ *4*

Pancakes............................................................8

Chia Pudding.......................................................10

Quinoa Fruit Salad ................................................12

Cinnamon Raisin Granola .......................................14

Banoffee Pie Pudding Cups .....................................17

Grain-Free Granola ...............................................19

Waffles ..............................................................22

Sun-Dried Tomato and Egg Muffin Cups ....................24

Sausage-Egg Muffin Cups .......................................26

Perfect Hash Browns..............................................28

Vegetable Skillet Hash with Eggs .............................30

Double White Chocolate Chip Brownies .....................32

Orange Ginger Glazed Turnips..................................35

White Chocolate Brownies.......................................37

Turnip Fries.........................................................40

Almond Butter Swirl Brownies .................................42

Roasted Toasted Garlic Shitake ................................45

Chocolate Strawberry Cupcakes ...............................47

Sweet Yam Roll ....................................................50

Orange Squares ....................................................53

Sicilian Salad .......................................................56

White Chocolate Chip Cookies ........................... 59

Garlic Aioli ........................................................ 62

Cinnamon Rice Crispy Treats ........................... 64

Rosemary Crackers .......................................... 66

Almond Butter Cookies .................................... 68

Crunchy Pineapple Cinnamon Flips .................. 70

Vanilla Pumpkin Bars ....................................... 72

Gluten Free Tortillas ........................................ 75

Caramel Almond Cake....................................... 78

Chili Pulled Pork Tacos ..................................... 80

*Conclusion* ...................................................... *82*

# Introduction

Did you know that your gut has trillions of bacteria, viruses, and fungal organisms—and that's a good thing! These organisms, collectively referred to as the microbiome, help you digest food, regulate metabolism, moderate your immune system, quell inflammation, remove toxins, and ensure efficient elimination.

A proliferation of "bad" bacteria due to chronic stress, the overuse of antibiotics, or a diet full of refined carbohydrates will result in an imbalanced microbiome. So, too, will inadequate "good" bacteria due to eating a diet without much fiber or probiotics.

It can be challenging it can be to cook healthy meals that satisfy the dietary preferences of the entire family while maintaining a reasonable food budget—it's a tall order. And, although I love spending time in the kitchen, I also love finding shortcuts to healthy meals so I can spend that extra time playing with my kids or simply enjoying the meal.

Here are ten tips that have worked for me and my family:

**1. Keep it simple.**

Pick recipes that involve five or fewer ingredients, or those that can be made in one pot. Also, look for recipes that don't require you to "transform" the ingredient. For example, peach chutney is delicious, but a simple uncooked peach salsa is even easier and saves you 30 minutes of cooking time.

**2. Plan meals ahead of time**

I keep a list of my family's favorite meals and add to it when I find recipes, we all enjoy. When it is time to plan each week's menu, I reach for that list first for most of the meal ideas, and then use cookbooks, magazines, or the farmers' market to inspire one or two new recipes each week. After that, I find I can do just one grocery shopping trip for the week and have healthy, fresh foods all week long. I also post the list of dinners on the refrigerator, and then we pick and choose based on the shelf life of produce or whatever we're feeling like that day.

**3. Make the bulk bins your new best friend.**

Chickpeas, lentils, 10-bean soup, and other bulk dried legumes make inexpensive, healthy, and filling meals.

**4. Get a jump-start on lunch prep.**

I typically grocery shop on Fridays or early Saturday mornings. This gives me the entire weekend to leisurely prepare foods for the kids' lunches. I like to mix up a big batch of trail mix, clean and cut carrots and celery, and make a batch or two of gluten-free cookies. It makes the weekday morning rush much more manageable! I recently invested in lunch boxes with resealable individual compartments—no more wasted sandwich bags or leaking containers.

**5. Build tradition into your weekly routine.**

For a long time, we enjoyed family pizza night every Friday. When summer rolled around, it became family grill night. The more meals you can put on autopilot, the easier life will be. Other options include Tuesday taco night, meatless Mondays, and breakfast for dinner any night. Just pick the foods your family loves and set up a standing date every week.

# Pancakes

These pancakes are made from a Whole-Grain Gluten-Free Flour Blend is built on a combination of whole-grain sorghum, whole-grain millet, and whole-grain brown rice flours, with a small amount of potato and tapioca starches for improved texture and browning.

**Serves:** 4

**Time:** 15 mins.

**Ingredients:**

- 1½ cups Whole-Grain Gluten-Free Flour Blend

- 1 tablespoon sugar
- 2 teaspoons aluminum-free, double-acting baking powder
- ¼ teaspoon sea salt
- 2 eggs
- 1 to 1½ cups milk
- 3 tablespoons canola oil
- 1 teaspoon vanilla extract

**Directions:**

1. Combine the flour blend, sugar, baking powder, and salt.

2. Whisk together your milk, eggs, vanilla and canola oil. Add in your milk mixture into the flour mixture and whisk to break up any lumps.

3. Set a nonstick skillet to get hot on medium heat.

4. With a ¼-cup measuring cup, ladle the batter onto the hot griddle. Cook the top until bubbles rise in the center of the pancakes and the edges set (for about 2 minutes).

5. Flip then allow the opposite side to cook (about 2 more minutes). Repeat with the remaining batter.

# Chia Pudding

This recipe is a favorite of athletes and have been for millennia.

**Serves:** 4

**Time:** 30 mins.

**Ingredients:**

- 2 cups unsweetened almond milk
- ⅔ cup chia seeds

- 2 tablespoons maple syrup

- 1 teaspoon vanilla extract

- Sliced fresh pears, for serving

- Cacao nibs, for garnish (optional)

**Directions:**

1. Whisk the vanilla, maple syrup, chia seeds and almond milk until thoroughly mixed. Cover and refrigerate for 25 minutes, or overnight.

2. Serve with sliced pears and garnish with cacao nibs (if using).

# Quinoa Fruit Salad

Eating whole grains for breakfast is healthy, because they are loaded with protein and complex carbohydrates.

**Serves:** 4

**Time:** 50 mins.

**Ingredients:**

- 1 cup quinoa, rinsed and drained
- 2 cups water
- Pinch sea salt

- Zest of 1 lime
- Juice of 1 lime
- 2 cups green grapes, halved
- 1 cup fresh strawberries
- 1 cup fresh blueberries
- 4 fresh mint leaves, thinly sliced

**Directions:**

1. Set a pot on medium heat, combine the quinoa, water, and salt. Allow to a simmer and switch to a low heat.

2. Cover and cook until fluffy (about 20 minutes). Switch off the heat and fluff with a fork.

3. Stir in the lime zest and juice, grapes, strawberries, and blueberries. Chill for 20 minutes or until ready to serve.

4. Just before serving, stir in the mint leaves.

# Cinnamon Raisin Granola

This Cinnamon Raisin Granola is homemade and much healthier than most breakfast cereals.

**Serves:** 8 cups

**Time:** 30 mins.

**Ingredients:**

- 6 cups gluten-free oats
- 1 tsp. vanilla extract

- 1 cup sliced toasted almonds (optional)
- ⅛ tsp. sea salt
- ¼ cup canola oil
- 2 tsps. ground cinnamon
- ¼ cup maple syrup
- 1 cup raisins

**Directions:**

1. Preheat the oven to 325°F.

2. Stir together the almonds and oats.

3. In a large measuring cup, whisk the cinnamon, salt, vanilla, maple syrup and canola oil.

4. The ingredients will not emulsify but do your best to combine them. Cover your oats with the liquid mixture then stir to coat.

5. Spread the oats over a baking sheet. Bake for 15 minutes. Stir thoroughly then bake for 5 minutes more.

6. Stir again. Continuing baking 5 more minutes, the mixture should be golden brown.

7. Cool the mixture completely before stirring in the raisins.

Enjoy!

# Banoffee Pie Pudding Cups

These delicious little puddings are inspired by raw, vegan "cheesecake" recipes and the British dessert banoffee pie.

**Serves:** 4

**Time:** 5 mins.

**Ingredients:**

- 1 cup raw cashews
- 2 ripe bananas
- ½ cup brewed coffee
- ¼ cup coconut oil, melted
- 1 teaspoon vanilla extract
- Pinch sea salt

**Directions:**

1. Add all your ingredients in your blender then purée until very smooth.

2. Evenly divide the mixture among 4 ramekins or small glass jars. Enjoy immediately.

# Grain-Free Granola

This recipe is completely grain-free and has a similar texture to artisan granola.

**Serves:** 5 cups

**Time:** 30 mins.

**Ingredients:**

- ½ cup pitted Medjool dates
- ⅓ cup very hot water

- ¼ cup coconut oil, melted
- 2 teaspoons vanilla extract
- ⅛ teaspoon sea salt
- 1 cup walnuts
- 1 cup almonds
- 1 cup cashews
- 1 cup shredded unsweetened coconut
- 1 cup raisins

**Directions:**

1. Preheat the oven to 350°F.

2. In a medium bowl, cover the dates with the hot water and soak for 5 minutes.

3. Add the coconut oil, vanilla, and salt. Transfer the date mixture to a blender, or use an immersion blender, and purée until mostly smooth.

4. Combine your cashews, almonds and walnuts in your food processor. Pulse until coarsely chopped.

5. Add the coconut and pulse once or twice, just to integrate.

6. Pour in the date purée and pulse one or two more times or stir by hand with a spatula.

7. Spread on a baking sheet then set to bake for 10 minutes.

8. Use a spatula to flip the nut mixture, trying to keep pieces intact as if they were cookies or bars, and then bake for 10 minutes more.

9. Stir then return it to the oven for 5 minutes. Remove the pan from the oven and stir in the raisins.

10. Cool completely then serve.

# Waffles

These waffles make a delicious breakfast or brunch.

**Serves:** 4

**Time:** 25 mins.

**Ingredients:**

- 2 cups Whole-Grain Gluten-Free Flour Blend
- 1 tablespoon sugar

- 1 tablespoon aluminum-free, double-acting baking powder
- ¼ teaspoon sea salt
- 3 eggs
- ½ cup milk
- ½ cup (1 stick) butter, melted
- 1 teaspoon vanilla extract

**Directions:**

1. Combine the salt, baking powder, sugar and flour blend.

2. Whisk the vanilla, butter, milk and eggs. Pour your mixture into the flour mixture and whisk to break up any lumps.

3. Heat a waffle iron according the manufacturer's directions.

4. With a ¼-cup measuring cup, ladle the batter onto the hot waffle iron. Cook according to the waffle iron manufacturer's instructions.

5. Transfer to a heatproof plate in a warm oven until ready to serve. Repeat with the remaining batter.

# Sun-Dried Tomato and Egg Muffin Cups

These muffin cups are especially helpful on long trips because gluten-free food is difficult to find at roadside restaurants.

**Serves:** 6

**Time:** 20 mins.

**Ingredients:**

- 12 eggs
- ½ teaspoon sea salt

- 1½ cups shredded fresh spinach
- ½ cup minced oil-packed sun-dried tomatoes
- ½ cup minced red onion
- ½ cup shredded Parmesan cheese (optional)

**Directions:**

1. Set your oven to preheat to 350°F.

2. Line a 12-cup muffin tin with paper liners.

3. In a large liquid measuring cup or juice pitcher, whisk the eggs and salt thoroughly.

4. Evenly divide the spinach, tomatoes, and onion among the 12 muffin cups.

5. Sprinkle each with an equal amount of Parmesan cheese (if using).

6. Pour the egg mixture evenly among the muffin cups to fill. Bake for 15 minutes or until set.

7. Cool for 5 minutes before serving.

# Sausage-Egg Muffin Cups

These are delicious with crumbled Italian gluten-free sausages.

**Serves:** 6

**Time:** 20 mins.

**Ingredients:**

- 12 eggs
- ½ teaspoon sea salt
- 12 ounces cooked, crumbled gluten-free sausage
- ½ cup minced red onion

- ¼ cup minced fresh basil (optional)

**Directions:**

1. Det your oven to preheat the oven to 350°F and prepare a muffin tin by lining with paper liners.

2. In a large liquid measuring cup or juice pitcher, whisk the eggs and salt thoroughly.

3. Evenly divide the sausage and onion among the 12 muffin cups.

4. Sprinkle with the basil (if using).

5. Divide evenly among in your muffin cups to fill. Bake for 15 minutes or until set.

6. Cool for 5 minutes before serving.

# Perfect Hash Browns

These hash browns are healthier than store-brought versions and can be made in just minutes at home.

**Serves:** 4

**Time:** 15 mins.

**Ingredients:**

- 2 large Russet potatoes, unpeeled, scrubbed, grated
- 2 tablespoons canola oil

- Sea salt
- Freshly ground black pepper

**Directions:**

1. Working with a handful of potatoes at a time, wring out the excess moisture.

2. Heat a large skillet or sauté pan on high heat with canola oil and tilt the pan to coat thoroughly. Heat for at least 30 seconds, but do not let it smoke.

3. Sprinkle the potatoes over the entire surface of the hot pan and season with salt and pepper.

4. Cook the potatoes, undisturbed, for 5 to 7 minutes to develop a deep golden-brown crust on the bottom.

5. If the bottom is cooking too quickly, lower the heat to medium.

6. Use a metal spatula to flip the hash browns. Cook the other side for 3 to 5 minutes until golden brown and cooked through. Serve immediately.

# Vegetable Skillet Hash with Eggs

This Vegetable Skillet Hash with Eggs has a healthy upgrade with sweet potatoes, zucchini, and bell peppers.

**Serves:** 4

**Time:** 30 mins.

**Ingredients:**

- 2 tablespoons canola oil, divided
- 2 small sweet potatoes, peeled and diced
- 1 small zucchini, diced

- bell pepper, 1, red, thinly sliced, cored
- ½ red onion, thinly sliced
- Sea salt
- Freshly ground pepper
- 4 eggs

**Directions:**

1. Heat a large sauté pan on high heat until hot. Add a half of your oil and tilt the pan to coat.

2. Add in your sweet potatoes then cook for 5 minutes.

3. Push the sweet potatoes to the side of the pan and add the zucchini. Sauté for 2 to 3 minutes.

4. Stir in your bell pepper and onion. Sauté for 2 to 3 minutes.

5. Stir everything together, adjust seasoning, and continue cooking until the sweet potatoes are soft, about 5 minutes more. Transfer the vegetables to a serving dish.

6. Add in your remaining oil then cook the eggs sunny-side up, or to your liking. Serve the eggs over the hash.

# Double White Chocolate Chip Brownies

This recipe for brownies is very versatile – feel free to add a sprinkle of white chocolate chips.

**Serves:** 8

**Time:** 45 minutes

## Ingredients:

- 5 ounces semisweet baking chocolate, chopped
- ½ cup vegetable shortening
- 2 large eggs
- 1 cup light brown sugar, packed
- ½ cup plus 2 tablespoons almond flour
- ¼ cup sorghum flour
- 1 tablespoon tapioca flour
- ½ teaspoon salt
- ¼ teaspoon baking soda
- 2 teaspoons vanilla extract
- 1 cup white chocolate chips

## Directions:

1. Set your oven to preheat to 350F then grease a 9x11-inch baking pan.

2. Melt the chocolate and shortening in a double boiler over low heat. Remove from heat and stir smooth.

3. Whisk your eggs and sugar until smooth.

4. Whisk in the melted chocolate mixture in small batches and beat until the mixture is smooth and well combined.

5. Stir together your baking soda, salt, tapioca, sorghum flour, and almond flour.

6. Fold in your dry ingredients until smooth.

7. Add in your vanilla then fold in the marshmallows.

8. Add your batter in your pan then smooth the top with a spatula.

9. Bake for 35 minutes until the brownies are set in the center – do not overcook.

10. Let the brownies to cool completely on a wire rack before cutting. Enjoy!

# Orange Ginger Glazed Turnips

For those of you loving turnips and vegetables next to your steaks, here you have the best of both worlds.

**Ingredients**

- 1 Pound Turnips - peeled and cut into 1/2" slices
- 1 Cup Water
- 1 Dash Sea Salt
- 1 Tablespoon Lard or Bacon Fat
- 1 Orange – save both the juice and zest
- 2 Tablespoons Raw Honey
- 1/2 Teaspoon Ground Ginger
- Ground Black Pepper

**Directions**

1. Place the salt and the water in a saucepan.

2. Add the turnips and bring the water to boil.

3. Next, switch the heat to low and simmer for 5 minutes until turnips are soft.

4. Drain the water.

5. Add the remaining ingredients (orange, honey and ginger) to the pan.

6. Stir to combine and sauté for 2-3 minutes until turnips are very soft and the glaze is slightly thicker.

7. Add salt and pepper to taste. Enjoy.

# White Chocolate Brownies

These white chocolate brownies may be just the treat you've been looking for!

**Serves:** 8

**Time:** 38 minutes

**Ingredients:**

- Rice flour (¾ cup)
- Potato starch (½ cup)

- Cornstarch (½ cup)

- xanthan gum (1/2 tsp.)

- Baking powder (1 tsp.)

- Salt (½ tsp.)

- Butter (½ cup, unsalted, softened)

- White sugar (¾ cup)

- Brown sugar (¾ cup, light, packed)

- Eggs (2 large)

- Vanilla (2 tsp.)

- White chocolate chips (1 cup)

**Directions:**

1. Set your oven to preheat to 350Fand grease a 9x13-inch baking pan.

2. Combine the salt, baking powder, xanthan gum, potato starch and rice flour in a mixing bowl.

3. Whisk your sugar and butter until fluffy.

4. Add the vanilla and eggs then beat until smooth.

5. Beat in the dry ingredients in small batches until smooth and well combined.

6. Fold in the white chocolate chips then spread the batter in the prepared pan.

7. Bake until the blondies are set (about 28 minutes).

8. Cool completely and serve.

# Turnip Fries

Turnips are low in calories, high in nutrients, and makes for the perfect snack.

## Ingredients

- turnip, 1, large, trimmed, cut into fries
- olive oil. 1 tablespoon
- Sea salt (1 tsp.)
- black pepper (1 tsp.)
- Paprika (1/2 tsp.)

**Directions**

1. Set oven to preheat to 400 degrees Fahrenheit.

2. Peel turnip with a potato peeler.

3. Evenly distribute fries onto a cookie sheet, being careful not to overlap.

4. Sprinkle with olive oil.

5. Sprinkle with sea seasonings.

6. Set to bake until done (about 20 minutes). Enjoy!

# Almond Butter Swirl Brownies

Almond butter and chocolate are two flavors that go well together.

**Serves:** 6

**Cook Time:** 35 minutes

**Ingredients:**

- ½ cup coconut flour
- ½ cup unsweetened cocoa powder
- ½ teaspoon baking soda
- ½ teaspoon salt

- 5 large eggs, lightly beaten
- 1/3 cup coconut oil, melted
- 2/3 cup honey
- 2 tablespoons coconut milk
- 1 teaspoon vanilla extract
- ¼ cup smooth almond butter

**Directions:**

1. Set your oven to preheat to 350Fand grease a square baking pan with cooking spray.

2. Whisk together the salt, baking soda, cocoa powder and coconut flour in a mixing bowl.

3. In a separate mixing bowl, blend the vanilla, coconut milk, honey, coconut oil and eggs.

4. Combine the wet and dry ingredients then blend well to combine.

5. Transfer to your prepared pan and tap it lightly on the counter a few times to release any air bubbles.

6. Microwave the almond butter for 10 to 15 seconds on high heat until melted.

7. Stir the almond butter smooth then drizzle over the brownie batter – gently swirl the almond butter into the batter with a butter knife.

8. Bake the brownies for 25 minutes or so until the center is set – do not over-bake.

9. Let the brownies cool completely before cutting.

# Roasted Toasted Garlic Shitake

This delicious dish works well as an entrée when paired with toast or mash, or as a snack when on its own.

**Serves:** 6

**Time:** 40 mins.

**Ingredients**

- Shitake Mushroom (1 lb.)
- Olive oil (2 tbsp.)
- Balsamic vinegar (1 tbsp.)
- Garlic (5 cloves, minced)
- Thyme (3 p, dried)

- Cayenne pepper (1.2 Pinches)
- Salt (¼ tsp.)
- Pepper (¼ tsp., cracked)
- Parsley (2 tbsp., chopped)

**Directions**

1. Set the oven to preheat to 400F.

2. Wipe the mushroom clean.

3. Leave them whole and only cut them if they are large.

4. Combine the pepper, olive oil, salt, garlic, cayenne and balsamic vinegar.

5. Coat the mushrooms with this mixture.

6. Place mushrooms on a baking sheet.

7. Roast in oven for 20-30 minutes.

8. Serve with fresh parsley.

# Chocolate Strawberry Cupcakes

These perfect cupcakes are made with rich chocolate flavor and fresh strawberries.

**Serves:** 12

**Time:** 30 minutes

**Ingredients:**

- ½ cup sorghum flour
- 1 cup fresh strawberries
- 1/3 cup tapioca flour
- ½ cup millet flour
- 1 tsp. xanthan gum
- 1/3 cup potato starch
- ¼ cup unsweetened cocoa powder
- ¼ tsp. sea salt
- ½ cup whole milk
- 3 tablespoons canola oil
- ½ cup warm water
- ½ tsp. baking powder
- 2 large eggs, beaten
- 1 tsp. vanilla extract
- 1 ½ tsp. baking soda

**Directions:**

1. Set your oven to preheat to 350F and line a muffin pan with paper liners.

2. Combine the salt, baking powder, baking soda, xanthan gum, cocoa powder, potato starch and flours then add to a mixing bowl.

3. Whisk together the water, eggs, vanilla and canola oil.

4. Combine both containers of ingredients – beat on high speed for 2 minutes.

5. Mash your strawberries gently with a fork. Fold the strawberries into the batter.

6. Spoon the batter into pan evenly.

7. Bake until done (about 20 minutes )

8. Cool the cupcakes completely. Top with icing and extra strawberries.

# Sweet Yam Roll

Here you have the ultimate bread-like recipe to go with your favorite slow cooked dinner.

**Serves:** 4

**Time:** 45 minutes

**Ingredients**

- Sweet Yam, 1/2 Cup, Cooked
- Almond Flour, Blanched, 1/4 Cup

- Tapioca Flour, 1 1/2 Cups

- Baking Powder, 1 tsp.

- Sea Salt, 1 tsp.

- 1/4 Cup Almond Milk

- Olive Oil, 1/4 Cup

- 1 Large Egg

- 1 Tablespoon Ghee (Optional)

**Directions**

1. Heat oven to 400 degrees F.

2. Combine the almond flour with the tapioca flour, the baking powder and the sea salt in a bowl. Make sure they have no clumps. Set aside.

3. Combine the olive oil, almond milk, cooked yam and egg in a separate bowl. Mix on low speed, with a mixer, until well blended.

4. To this, slowly add half of the flour mixture from the first bowl. Mix the dough with your hands adding the remaining half the flour until gone. Knead for 2 minutes until it stops being sticky. Cover and set aside for 10 minutes.

5. Roll the dough out into equal balls and place on a baking sheet covered with parchment paper. Bake in the oven for 14-17 minutes and the tops get light brown.

6. Allow to cool for 15-20 minutes.

7. Serve

# Orange Squares

Full of fresh orange flavor, these orange squares are soft and tender.

**Serves:** 8

**Time:** 15 minutes + chilling

**Ingredients:**

**For the Crust Layer:**

- ¾ cup chopped almonds
- ¼ cup unsweetened shredded coconut
- 5 pitted medjool dates
- 2 ½ teaspoons fresh orange zest
- ¼ teaspoon salt

**For the Top Layer:**

- 1/3 cup coconut oil
- 2 tablespoons honey
- 2 tablespoons fresh orange juice
- 1 teaspoon fresh orange zest
- 3 drops liquid stevia

**Directions:**

1. Combine the almonds, coconut, dates, salt and orange zest for the crust layer in a food processor until well combined.

2. Transfer into the bottom of a square glass dish that has been lined with parchment paper, spreading evenly.

3. Beat the coconut oil in a mixing bowl until creamy.

4. Add the orange juice, orange zest, honey and liquid stevia and blend until smooth.

5. Spread the mixture over top of the crust layer then cover with plastic and chill for 1-2 hours minutes or until set.

6. Remove the parchment paper and cut into squares.

7. Serve cold topped with a shake of icing sugar or coconut.

# Sicilian Salad

Easy, simple and gluten-free.

**Serves:** 3

**Time:** 10 minutes

**Ingredients:**

- 1 Lemon, juiced
- Black Pepper, 1 tsp., ground
- Garlic, 1 Clove, Minced
- Red Pepper Flakes, ¼ Tsp
- Lacinato Kale, 1 Bunch

- Oregano, ½ Tsp, Dried
- Olive Oil, 3 Tbsp
- Sea Salt, ¼ Tsp

**Topping:**

- Pepperoncini, ½ Cup
- ¼-½ Lb. Hard Salami, Diced
- Roasted Cauliflower (optional)
- ½ Cup Pickled Sweet Peppers or Cherry Tomatoes
- 4-6 Marinated Artichoke Hearts
- ¼ Cup Green Olives
- Red Onion Slices Rings, 6 Pickled (optional)
- ¼ Cup Toasted Sunflower Seeds

**Directions**

1. Combine your salt, pepper, oregano, olive oil, lemon juice and red pepper flakes.

2. Close with the lid and blend it by shaking vigorously.

3. Slice kale leaves thinly and toss them in a bowl.

4. Coat kale with the lemon dressing.

5. Combine the remaining 8 ingredients to create topping.

6. Place kale in individual salad bowls.

7. Sprinkle topping over the kale.

# White Chocolate Chip Cookies

Finally, fresh cookies everyone can enjoy!

**Serves:** 12

**Time:** 25 minutes

**Ingredients:**

- ¾ cup potato starch
- 1 ½ cups brown sugar, packed
- ½ cup almond flour

- 1 cup sorghum flour
- ½ teaspoon salt
- 1 teaspoon xanthan gum
- 2/3 cup canola oil
- 1 teaspoon baking soda
- 2 large eggs
- ¾ cup semisweet white chocolate chips
- 3 teaspoons vanilla extract

**Directions:**

1. Combine your dry ingredients in a bowl.

2. Whisk your vanilla, eggs and oil in a separate bowl then beat into the dry ingredients until smooth and well combined.

3. Fold in the white chocolate chips then cover and chill the dough for 45 to 60 minutes.

4. Set the oven to preheat to 350F and line a baking sheet with foil.

5. Shape the dough into 1-inch balls and arrange them on the baking sheet.

6. Lightly flatten each cookie and bake for 12 to 14 minutes, turning half way, until golden on the edges but still soft to the touch.

7. Let the cookies cool in the pan for 3 to 5 minutes then allow to cool completely. Enjoy.

# Garlic Aioli

This garlicky mayonnaise is delicious and easy to whip up.

**Serves:** ½ cup

**Time:** 5 mins.

**Ingredients:**

- Egg, 1 yolk
- lemon juice, 1 tsp.
- garlic, 1 small clove, minced
- olive oil, 2 tbsp., extra-virgin

- canola oil, ⅓ cup

**Directions:**

1. Whisk the garlic, lemon juice and egg yolk until integrated.

2. Whisking constantly, slowly drizzle in the olive oil a few drops at a time.

3. Continuing to whisk constantly to emulsify, slowly drizzle in the canola oil a few drops at a time until thick and pale.

4. Refrigerate, covered, for up to 3 days.

# Cinnamon Rice Crispy Treats

These cinnamon rice crispy treats are simple to throw together and delicious.

**Serves:** 6

**Time:** 15 minutes

**Ingredients:**

- ½ cup agave nectar
- 1 tbsp. cinnamon powder
- ¾ cup natural almond butter
- 2 tablespoons coconut oil

- 1 ½ teaspoons vanilla extract
- 6 cups gluten-free rice cereal

**Directions:**

1. Line your baking pan and set aside.

2. Add your agave nectar, and cinnamon to a saucepan on medium heat, stir, allow to melt and bubble slowly.

3. Switch off the heat then stir in your vanilla, coconut oil and almond butter.

4. Stir the mixture gently until it thickens slightly.

5. Pour your cereal in a large bowl then top with your agave mixture.

6. Gently stir the cereal until it is evenly coated then press it into the prepared pan, spreading it evenly.

7. Cover the pan with plastic and chill until the bars are firm. Cut to serve.

# Rosemary Crackers

These rosemary crackers have a fine aroma and is delicious.

**Serves:** 12

**Time:** 25 minutes

**Ingredients**

- 1 Tablespoon Olive Oil
- 2 Cups Almond Flour
- 1/2 Teaspoon Sea Salt
- 2 Tablespoons Rosemary
- 1/4 Teaspoon Coconut Oil
- 2 Tablespoons Water
- 1 Egg White

## Directions

1. Preheat oven to 350 degrees F.

2. Combine salt, almond flour and rosemary in a medium bowl.

3. Combine the coconut oil (melted), water, olive oil, and egg white. Whisk ingredients together.

4. Transfer your egg mixture to your flour mixture then stir until a dough forms.

5. Add water or oil only if it doesn't stick together as a dough ball.

6. Roll dough between parchment paper to an even thickness of 1/4 inch thick.

7. Add your parchment to a baking pan then discard the top parchment.

8. Bake for 10 minutes, let them set in the oven for 10 minutes with the heat turned off.

9. Great when served with Hummus.

# Almond Butter Cookies

These cookies are easy to make and tasty.

**Serves:** 12

**Time:** 25 minutes

**Ingredients:**

- white sugar, ¾ cup
- baking soda, 1 tsp.
- vanilla extract, ½ tsp.
- 1 pinch salt
- Egg, 1 large

- natural almond butter, 1 cup, smooth

## Directions

1. Set your oven to preheat to 350F and line a baking pan.

2. Beat together the sugar, baking soda, vanilla extract, salt and egg in a mixing bowl until smooth.

3. Add the almond butter and beat until well combined.

4. Drop the dough in rounded teaspoons onto the prepared baking sheet and lightly flatten with the back of a fork.

5. Bake for 10 minutes, turning half way, or until the cookies are just set.

6. Leave on the tray to set for 10 minutes, then cool and serve.

# Crunchy Pineapple Cinnamon Flips

There's nothing quite like the amazing flavor of cinnamon and pineapples.

**Serves:** 6

**Time:** 25 minutes

**Ingredients**

- 1-2 Pineapples
- 1 Tsp. Cinnamon

## Directions

1. Preheat oven to 200 degrees F.

2. Slice the pineapple into very thin slices and take out the seeds.

3. Line the slices on a baking sheet covered in parchment paper.

4. Leave space between the slices.

5. Sprinkle with cinnamon.

6. Bake the slices for 1 hour, then flip them over.

7. Continue baking and flipping for 1-2 hours, until they're dry throughout.

8. Cool and enjoy.

# Vanilla Pumpkin Bars

These Vanilla Pumpkin Bars full of flavor, and moist.

**Serves:** 12

**Time:** 1 Hour 25 minutes

**Ingredients:**

- 1 cup Almond Flour
- 1 Banana Mashed
- 1 Cup of Pumpkin Puree
- 1/2 Cup Organic Honey
- 2 Tsp Vanilla

- 2 Tbsp Water
- 1 Free Range Egg
- 3/4 tsp Sea Salt
- Spray Oil

**Directions**

1. Pre-heat Oven to 350F

2. Line a baking dish (a square one preferably) with parchment and spray with oil.

3. Mix the egg, banana, pumpkin, water and honey together in a bowl.

4. Mix the almond flour, sea salt and vanilla together in a separate bowl.

5. Pour the pumpkin mixture in to the almond mixture and blend well.

6. Pour the combined mixture in to the lined baking dish.

7. Bake for an hour and check, it could take a little longer.

8. My cooking times have varied between 55mins and 1hour and 10 minutes so keep an eye on your oven - It should be golden and a crust should be visible on top.

9. Switch off the oven when done then cool in the dish for 10 minutes before moving to a wire rack.

10. Cut in to 9 pieces, they are nice served warm or cold.

# Gluten Free Tortillas

These tasty tortillas are perfect for Taco Tuesdays.

**Serves:** 2

**Time:** 25 minutes

**Ingredients**

- Almond Flour, 1 Cup, Blanched
- Tapioca Flour 1 Cup
- ½ Tsp. Sea Salt
- Olive Oil, 4 Tbsp., Light
- Warm Water, 6 Tbsp.

**Directions**

1. Dip the measuring cup into the almond flour and scrape the top, to make sure you get exactly 1 cup.

2. Whisk together the almond flour, tapioca and sea salt.

3. Add oil to the flour mixture and stir until the flour is blended thoroughly.

4. Add the water to the bowl and stir until well combined.

5. On a flat surface, knead the dough for 1 minute.

6. Divide into 8 pieces and knead each well for about 30 seconds.

7. Roll each piece into a ball.

8. Keep them covered with a towel between uses.

9. Place a ball between two pieces of parchment paper.

10. Flatten with a rolling pin.

11. Cook in a skillet for a minute.

12. Flip then cook for another minute.

13. Use with any recipe calling for tortillas.

# Caramel Almond Cake

This delicious cake is moist and hassle-free.

**Serves:** 8

**Time:** 8 Minutes

**Ingredients**

- 2 oz. butter (soft)
- 5 oz. sugar
- 1 cup almond flour
- baking powder, 1 tsp.
- ¼ tsp. baking soda
- Salt, ¼ tsp.
- 1 tsp. vanilla

- 1 egg
- 1 cup Greek yogurt, caramel (full fat)

## Directions

1. Grease a 9-inch layer cake tin and sprinkle with a little almond flour. Heat oven to 375 degrees F.

2. Sift your salt, baking soda, baking powder, almond flour, and sugar in a large bowl. Stir to combine and set aside.

3. Place in a blender, egg, butter, sugar, banana, and vanilla. Blend for 1 minute at super speed; consistency should be smooth.

4. Pour blended mixture into almond flour mixture and mix thoroughly.

5. Pour and scrape into greased tin. Place in oven and bake for 25 mins. Cool and serve.

# Chili Pulled Pork Tacos

Whoever said you needed gluten to make tacos, have obviously never tried this delicious recipe.

**Serves:** 10 servings

**Time:** 8 hours

**Ingredients:** -

- Pork butt / shoulder (4 ½ lbs.)
- Chili powder (2 tbsp.)
- Kosher salt (1 tbsp.)
- Ground cumin (1 ½ tsp.)
- Ground oregano (½ tsp.)

- Crushed red pepper flakes (¼ tsp.)
- Pinch ground cloves
- Stock or broth (½ cup)
- Bay leaf (1)

**Directions:**

1. Combine oregano, chili powder, cumin, salt, cloves and red pepper flakes in a mixing bowl.

2. Clean and wash pork and put it on a clean platter. Rub spice mix thoroughly on all sides of the pork using your hands.

3. Allow to marinate overnight for at least two hours in the refrigerator.

4. Place in slow cooker with stock/broth and bay leaf. Set on low for a period of 8 hours.

5. When completed, separate from liquid and place pork on a cutting board. Use 2 forks to shred meat.

6. Serve in butter lettuce.

# Conclusion

You did it. Congrats on exploring all 30 Celiac recipes. All these recipes are easy to create and are extremely delicious.

Keep on practicing and sharing your creations with your loved ones. Be sure to leave your honest feedback on Amazon if you enjoyed what you read.

Cheers!

Printed in Great Britain
by Amazon

12291167R00047